4 YOU, DAUGHTER
Vol. 1

Believe In Yourself

By: Rayki Tai

New York, NY

2014

Believe In Yourself

Acknowledgements

Remi – You have changed my life in ways that you would never know. You are my inspiration. Thanks for letting me love you and loving me back.

Ashley – I've learned so much from you. You started it all and didn't even know it. You taught me love, strength, and determination. Without your love, I'd be nothing.

Hope – You set me up to succeed. You made sure to give me the tools of the trade and inadvertently showed me how to use them. I couldn't ask for a better angel.

Girl Power Publishing – Spectacular mission and I appreciate the support. When you love what you do, you never have to work a day in your life.

"I believe the children are our future. Teach them well and let them lead the way." – Whitney Houston

For you, my precious daughter, because a truly happy girl is a truly fulfilled woman.

Copyright © 2015 All rights reserved. Printed in the United States of America.

www.4youdaughter.com

Over the years, you'll celebrate birthdays and other special events. Today, I want to celebrate YOU!

I'm so proud to be your mother. Thank you for filling my world with more joy and love than I've ever known. You're a dream come true from heaven above.

Your love turned our house into a home.

No matter where you go,

you will never be alone.

Just believe in yourself the way I believe in you. Love yourself the way I love you and you will know love without limits.

No matter what life has to offer you, I'll be there every step of the way.

Dream Big.

Dream Often.

You are a born leader with natural talents. Never settle for being average. Aim for the top and work hard to get what you want.

Learn these important life lessons to guide you through the amazing life ahead of you:

Life's a journey.

Always enjoy the ride.

Think happy.

Stay happy.

Live life with laughter and love.

Give the gift of friendship whenever you can. Always show respect and consideration.

Pray. Be thankful for your blessings. Find comfort and peace in your faith.

Character is doing the right thing when nobody is looking.

The only person you should ever compete with is the person you were yesterday. Always strive to be the best version of YOU.

Reading is food for your brain. Don't starve yourself. Read on.

Don't try too hard to fit in when you were born to stand out.

Be different and dare to be you.

Be honest. Be sure to speak truth.

Be fearless; because there's no one quite like you.

Follow your passions and explore your talents.

Embrace your possibilities with open arms, an open mind, and an open heart.

Let your creativity run wild. Your mind is full of really great ideas.

If you focus, you will surely succeed…

in building the wealth to buy anything you need.

As I watch you grow, I see the world through your eyes and I have great hope for the future.

Stay focused. Stay organized.

Remember...

You always pass failure on your way to SUCCESS. So, don't ever give up!

Just in case you have to try
something alone, just do it.

Your **determination** and inner strength
is all you need.

But you can't just dream of your success. You have to work hard for it.

Turn
your
can'ts
into
cans

...and your dreams into plans.

Choose to be happy

even when you're feeling sad.

So turn a frown upside down because it's the right thing to do.

Others may try to dim your light, but shine on sunshine. You shine so bright.

The GOOD will always outweigh the bad so be grateful for all the good you have.

Then watch the GOOD mulitply and the bad subtract.

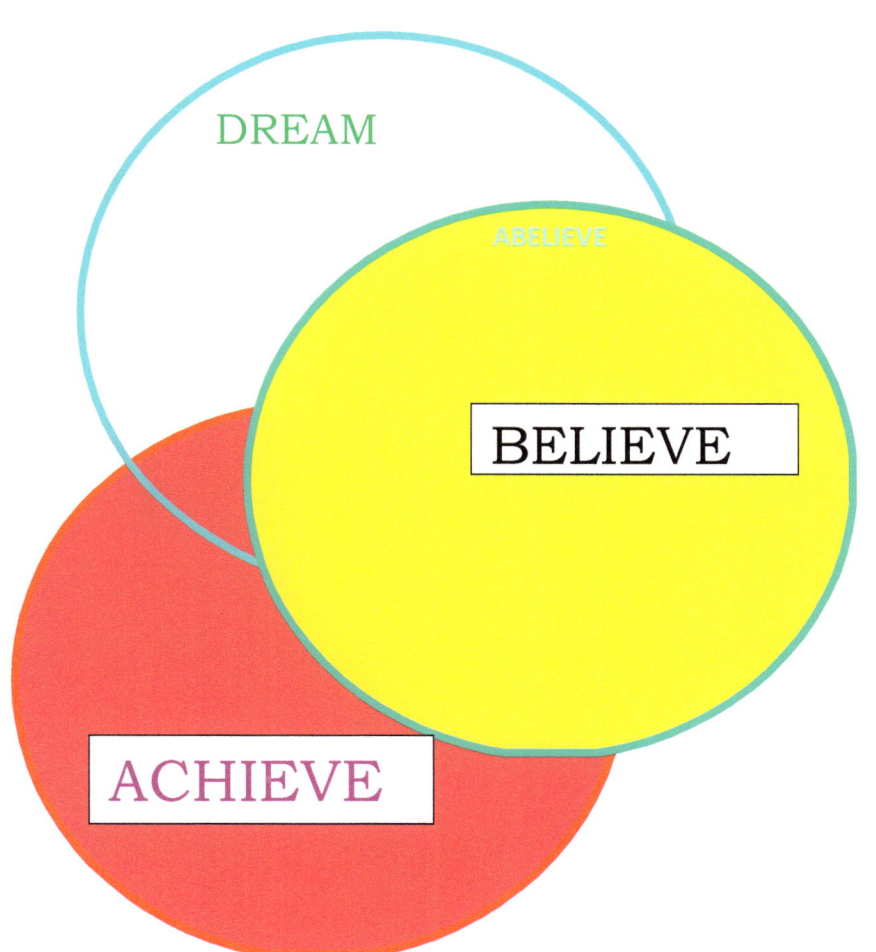

Believe it
and you'll
achieve it.
It's all up
to you.

Be BOLD… Be FREE.
Be free to be YOU.
Whatever you do, just unleash the
winner in you!

Step into
your
greatness
and
stand tall
in
success.

The world is yours. So, do what you want with it.

You get what you put in; so give it all you got. Aim for the stars. You have a really good shot.

I'm so excited to see what the future has in store for you!

4 my beautiful and precious daughter,

With all my love coming straight from the heart, I will love you tomorrow the way I did from the start. Place your hand in mine and I will hold you up high. Believe in yourself and the limit is the sky. Shine brighter than a diamond like the twinkle in your eye. Shine bright, shine bright. I know you'll do just fine.

I promise to LOVE you forever.

AUTHOR PAGE

Rayki Tai is a transformational author and speaker committed to empowering girls around the globe. She is a devoted mother of 2 beautiful daughters embarking on a lifelong global mission to motivate and inspire our daughters to realize their true potential. Rayki is an educator and a speaker transforming girls through her encouraging books and products. As a result, young girls are able to tap into their greatness and live productive lives filled with love and abundance.

www.4youdaughter.com

www.ingramcontent.com/pod-product-compliance
Lightning Source LLC
Chambersburg PA
CBHW041813040426
42450CB00001B/18